LITTLE BRO

Wildflowers
AND OTHER POEMS

BY CASSIDY ARKIN & SANDRA ROGERS-HARE

A Little Brown Girl Production, New York City NY
Ghenghis Khan Urban Guerrilla Research Society, a subsidiary of
Rogershare Publishers
San Leandro CA
2019

LITTLE BROWN GIRL

Wildflowers & other Poems...

by
Cassidy Arkin and Sandra Rogers-Hare

Wildflowers

Minnesota wildflowers
Daisies in central park
California poppy petals, Petaluma
We are all from somewhere
We are all wildflowers
Noticing makes the difference
Our poems volley between us
A spiral conversation
Cass and I are tied by an invisible cord
Since
Whenever
How old are we all, anyway?

- Sandra Rogers-Hare

...

AN INTRODUCTION

I was a member of the first generation of children born in a community called Synanon. Although it has since been described and discredited as a cult, for me, it was my home. My memories of the community are that it was a good place. When I was a kid I was endlessly fascinated with the outside world because we were forbidden to be part of it. My mother and I left when I was six years old. That was the first time I experienced the outside world, and I would soon learn that I was just one of many *Wildflowers* in the world. This book is the product of collaboration between my mother and me. Here, we take the opportunity to tell our story and encourage others to do the same. I give you, *Little Brown Girl: Wildflowers and other poems...*

...

LITTLE BROWN GIRL

Little Secret…
It's not "Little Brown Girl,"
It's what "Little Brown Girl" represents…
If it were, you'd have been writing it,
not talking about it.
Stay focused.
Don't blink.
xoxo
mom

- Sandra Rogers-Hare

THE UNEXAMINED LIFE IS NOT WORTH LIVING

SOCRATES, PHILOSOPHER

BIRTH

I was
a vision of the future…
Designed
with the knowledge
and cooperation of my community,
became the focus of commentary
and discussion
about what born
and bred
kids in my community could become.

It was
a foreign concept
but it is what defined
how I came to be.
Me,
a child born into a first-generation society,
to a community that would cease to exist.

I would never be able to return.

- Cassidy Arkin

WE ARE
AT OUR BEST WHEN WE ARE
FIGHTING
TO SURVIVE

SANDRA ROGERS-HARE

BEGINNINGS...

In the beginning there were...
Footsteps are all I can hear behind me,
Noises and laughter all I hear as I turn my head,
Faint, pungent, distinct scents, wildflowers
    and echoes of familiar chuckles playing
around the edge of my memory,
Glimmers of a light dancing in someone else's eyes.
It's all slow motion, my life in memory.
Moving faces warped, shaded, so three
dimensional that I can see the tiny scales and
wrinkles of those youthful faces,
as they move on
perhaps to a higher place in life.
I, in a way, remember my entire life,
then,
obliquely, not because it's felt,
       but because...
There was once a brown girl
a small
little girl...
known for her crackly voice and her loud,
vibrant self...
and this little girl,
went on a quest to understand her identity
and her place...
in this world.
The dichotomy brings both
disillusion and truth.

Little Brown Girl...

- *Cassidy Arkin*

THIS MORNING…

DEAR CASS, I met you early this morning, still dark, walking the dogs. I said, "Hi Cass, what're you doing here?" The response was, "I'm Cassidy's angel. She wants you to know she's always looking out for you."

- Sandra Rogers-Hare

UTOPIA

Purple, green tiled floors,
scraps of silver stuck in the black,
stained tile.
My teeth bright white.
I see you
and,
I have to catch my breath,
because I remember you and me,
and I can't move forward
or backward from that place.
I can't open my eyes... can only close them
my tears squeeze out between my lids,
they fall down,
my cheeks blush red, my skin,
brown and shining,
my eyes remembering us for the first time.
In a complex world, a mosaic.
You kissed me
Once
as you were leaving,
the room becomes yellow and bright,
and we see that your father,
your mother—were there too.
You're leaving me, running to open the door
to the cool, sharp, evil-minded world
that swallowed you, took you away.

You,
From that day forward, nothing was ever the same.
The breaking of love in that one motion.
I loved you,
and I do miss you,
Those moments lost...
to *Utopia*.

- *Cassidy Arkin*

THE SUN

She looked to the sun,
and gained energy,
there from...
It was one.
It was two.
Too... too much beauty
on this avenue.

- *Sandra Rogers-Hare*

WALLS

I know when the walls start to slowly close in
and darkness takes over
and I have no more energy...
I have to stay in the sunlight
until my joy comes home.

- *Cassidy Arkin*

SUN BURNISHES

Honey, you were made to fly. That feeling that
everything's up in the air? That the ground
done just fell away from under your feet? That
free fall? My thinking is, break the mold. You
have already, anyway. Just go to the part of the
planet where you can ride horses bareback, eat
sloppy, get some flanks, and let your hair fly
free. Go where the sun burnishes your skin and
fills you with vitamin D. Go where you are only
you and that is enough because there is a poem
a day inside you and a documentary on the
weekends. Break the bonds of slavery this
media industry has on you. That's
OPPORTUNITY!

- Sandra Rogers-Hare

BURNING.... in New York

Honey. Babe. I had a dream, of burning white bones.
The dream felt so real. It took me 'home' to a place I
haven't been in a long, long time—to my community.
We were in my apartment right here, but it was much
larger and roomier. I remember looking at my stove.
Smoke began to fill the kitchen. I could smell it—it was
like burning bones, and as the smoke proceeded to
flow, my body became numb. And you and our friends
slowly began to disappear. I struggled for the door as
everything around me, my apartment, my bedroom,
living room, all began to change form. This is where
the door finally opened. My hand was weak from
trying to open it. People were running out of the
building, out of the apartment complex, down the
steps and into the street. And I was frantic. "What's
going on? Does anyone know what's happening?"
Suddenly, one of my neighbors approached me, said
he saw white-smoke rising from within me, that it had
set my apartment building on fire. I freaked. "In me?" I
asked, as I gazed back at the standing figures.

I was standing there with the apartment building
behind me, which had in the process of all the turmoil,
transcended many feet high into a mountainous cube,
huge and beautiful, with deep red-brown walls,
curtains and windows that looked like they were out of
a magazine. In a flash I was inside my apartment. It was
all so amazing, 'amazing' because it wasn't my
apartment. I had never seen it before... I had never
seen anything so polished, perfect, beautiful. It was
like real-life, but it was a dream... my dream. I could
almost taste the strawberries and whipped cream and

the red wine. I was confused, and people from the building swarmed in. I tried to explain that this was not my apartment. That it had transcended into some foreign, picture-perfect home I had never seen before, yet they persisted sitting there on the floor, taking comfort, some kind of refuge within the walls of my so-called-apartment— home, yet I, I, found none, only distance, isolation and a deep feeling of loss. This was not my home. Yet the people, they sat on the floors, the couches, it was like a silent party, a wake, and the sun, its light strewn through the living room windows was so bright that it made way for daylight and motion. The local schools were filled with children and their cries. Their voices could be heard through the windows. The white smoke persisted, as did the smell, and I was cold, at a loss and fearful. This is when you appeared, yes you appeared, with friends, and the life of my soul came to, my eyes lit up, and my heart felt heavy. And this is where I finally understood, because right there, in that instant... I was breathing through you.

The smell of burning white bones grew heavier and heavier. Simultaneously, as my body lifted, as a result, of your presence, I felt a strain of sadness, because inside I knew, I knew that I would never be able to return... and I wanted that. Inside myself, I wept, and outside in this foreign apartment, the floors and the corners of the rooms became wet from my tears, damp and moist, cold, defunct. My surroundings mirrored my soul, my emotions were so heavy they affected the people around me, and though my visions were frightfully strong, I listened to you, but inside, my gut instinct knew—the truth... I had to let go. It is here that you gave me the promise of a home as I looked at a desk, a brown, small, messy, dark, maple desk where pictures lay, and there were photos of me of 'that' time. And within these photos, the story played out, and I was able to see each instance and setting of time recapture my life. For those few instances I was happy to see my community. I shuffled through a few more photos as you sat on your bed working, and looking for something. We were still in the apartment that was presumably mine and where people sat on floors and beds for no reason but to smell and feel the deadening of time, and the deepness... the bleeding of my heart. Yet in this foreign home, lies my past, strange and significant, and your life, and the fullness—of my heart.

THE STORY CONTINUES... and so it is there where I saw myself playing at six years old, writing my story in my backyard, feeling the pull of my past. Sitting on the ground with the sun high, I moved under a branch to be in the shade. And there, I saw myself bury it in the ground—me jabbing the smallest hole in the earth. I thought I would be able to save it... so that I could return to it whenever I felt it slipping away. This is where you grabbed the photo, trying to protect me from the truth ... "Protect?" ... it was too late ... and I could feel my body struggle ... my heart weep ... the room felt dead ... cold and icy ... the people sitting on the floor were no longer absorbing this energy, only watching us as though we were a part of a movie. I screamed and began to punch you ... yet my hits were light ... weightless ... you did nothing ... I was still hitting you ... my eyes ... filled-heavy-with-tears ... blurring my vision as I began to grab everything of mine in that small room ... and it was here the lingering scent fell stagnant ... there was nothing more there for me in that small room... I knew I had to go... and so, my bags were packed ... the door was open and I walked ... not once looking back... feeling the absence so great that hunger grew within me ... a hunger for the truth... and it was there ... and only there ... in this dream that I finally knew... that I had to keep going. In moments I was out on the street and in some foreign place... watching traffic zoom down a street and people ... tourists walking down and away from the apartment ... the white, smoke-filled home that smelt like burning bones and was dampened with increasing water ... my tears ... and it was there that I left my tears and was challenged with the open road ... the unknown ...

- *Cassidy Arkin*

CHUCK DEDERICH, FOUNDER OF SYNANON

DOPEFIEND...

Honey,
you have made an extraordinary connection in
your collective unconscious.
Been wanting to tell you this for years.
Dauphin... dauphine, to you means dopefiend.
Somehow you translated that out from what you
heard as a kid
Banging your head against the door in the
green room
Listening to the Wire.
While the cows moved slowly across the green
hills outside your windows
accompanied by the shouting and defending in
the Synanon Games.
But *dauphin* comes from the French,
it means *heir apparent*
well, literally, it also means *dolphin*
And comes from land ceded by the last
Dauphin de Viennois in
1337 to the French king on condition it be held
by his eldest son.
The last Dauphin to personally rule was the
Louis XI, until 1461.
Interesting connection for me because Synanon
was all about entitlement
Chuck Dederich was the King
And Jady was his heir apparent, the Dauphiné.
They tried to groom Chuck Jr. for the job
but he didn't have the charisma,
the leadership skills.
They said he was dumb,
but it was much more electric than that.
So, when you whip "dauphine" around like a
feather in the air.
You stir up memories about a kingdom from
long ago.

With counts and knights riding around on their
horses
Or motorcycles
Palace intrigue
Venal crimes
And murders in the night.

- Sandra Rogers-Hare

DON'T FUCK WITH
SYNAN⊖N
I THINK THAT'S THE NEW
RELIGIOUS POSTURE.

CHUCK DEDERICH, FOUNDER OF SYNANON

AT SUNRISE

Beautiful Sunrise…
I wonder where this life will take me
and where I will go…
knowing in my heart,
that there is a message…

- Cassidy Arkin

CRYING

Yes, I knew you were crying
But I could only hear a few words.
What was on your heart?

- Sandra Rogers-Hare

CLOUDS WENT DARK ......

I met you at the door,
your name was Love.
I asked you to come in
but you said...
I already am.
You kept returning and I kept opening the
door...
Looking at me
I didn't recognize you.
You said *Come with me*...
I looked away.
That night—I fell awake looking at the sky.
Clouds went dark.
Stars shined bright.
I felt you briefly,
and in that moment...
I dreamed awake.
Touch was so heavy,
so beautiful,
the night pulled me down.
Slept with me.
Love said....
Go there...
have patience
and if you're lucky...
God will let your dreams unfold...

- Cassidy Arkin

MIRACLES

Intuition tells me miracles
are happening
all the time.
Like sun rays,
They're falling on us all around.
Things just get in the way,
and we don't notice them.
Same for good things.
God is always good.

- Sandra Rogers-Hare

SILENCE

Fingers tied up,
Laughter painted on
And tears ever so long.
Silence is quite a friend...

- Cassidy Arkin

CONDUCIVE

"Conducive" is "conducive to...."
people are "who" not "that"
gaps are "between" not "for"
"collaboration" means many things to you,
but usually not
collaboration.
For you and me,
Verbalizing is not our primary language.
Our mother tongue is mad music,
catching a joke,
having an insight,
and growing a notch.
We speak words as if they were a foreign
vernacular
but in our overweening need to communicate,
We, you and I,
We master language and make it work for us!

- Sandra Rogers-Hare

RIDDLES

We live in laughter
Made of walls,
and
Jokes without a punch line...

- Cassidy Arkin

THE SYSTEM

Cass, if you are willing to collaborate, we can discover whole new insights about how to teach kids locked out of the system. This place has much more color, more depth for me now. Some of the teachers are extraordinary, so are some of the families. As always, it is a privilege to be with people of such indomitable spirit. Let me know what you want to do!

- Sandra Rogers-Hare

For NOTUGLY Clothing Campaign

ADAM & EVE
the story...

Eve,
Underneath it all I wore his underwear,
The red-pink-visual and urban-wear fit tight
and snug,
around the undercuts of my ass
and then to my thighs,
curvaceous and intruding is what my friends
use to say about my ass.
The perfect bombshell,
and so was I.

Now Adam on the other hand,
he was different.
My friends always wondered why and where
I could find such an outrageous looking cat,
but I loved him anyhow and anywhere.

And of course,
there were times when he would yell at me!
But God how I loved a good bark
and the aftermath
the make-up-break-up fight,
and session.
It was love!!!
Red-hot love on the strike,
where Adam would take me to the mountain,
and I would be carrying the Mic singing
and praising all the way to the top.
I guess this is how people started to call us
Adam and Eve's perfect equation.
We were eternal
wearing nothing but
NOTUGLY
and straight baby-fish skins.

And of course,
there were times when he would yell at me,
Adam that is
and fight with me,
but I didn't care.
We just fit!
Me and my perfect bombshell ass,
wearing "Good Girl's Pak"
and "Sugar's T-Top"
Adam,
he loved this.
The tightness of my clothes left his mouth dry,
inviting me to wet it and then turning it on
was like turning off the world
because as Adam would get up from the bed,
our bed that is...
wearing Notugly's fantasy of "Jesus loves me
too!" T-shirt,
it was as though Adam took on the presence of
Jesus and his look,
a beard, half shaven, darkly grim, but sexy.
I loved my Adam.
I truly loved him
and he used to wear my favorite shirt...
which would eventually end up on me.
It was our rumble and tumble moments and
then the shifty-tricky-shift.
He loved this maneuver,
"usuckwhat?"
the T-shirt would read...
and I would answer,
"naturally..."

The story of us,
Adam, and me, Eve,
is a super futuristic version of a great love story,

which we took a stake into
a WEAR on which we weren't used to.

One day,
Adam and I stood in the middle of Central Park
where nothing could be heard but the wind
and the sound of the trees blowing along
fall's winter shadow.
Adam got down on his knees and began to
speak,
"Will you notice me... Eve?"
PANIC!
I cried out,
loud and clear,
"Adam, I am blue-green in heaven's hell,"
What was that! I thought.
Thinking that this was his way of saying
that he was leaving me,
and that New York was now my living hell.

Again,
I screamed,
"Adam, please don't leave!"
Soundless whispers were heard
through the air
as people around, me appeared
wearing shirts inscribed with
"Red Light" and "Bless the Future."
I couldn't understand...
There I felt,
the ground shifting... like an earthquake,
Feeling the warmth of my Adam's breath,
his heart began to beat fast.
I had never seen this in him...

I grabbed my "Bad Girl's 3-Pak"
and immediately put it to his mouth so he could
breathe
my body clothed,

cottoned and well.
Adam could feel and place
the intensity of his world coming to.
He could feel something take over him.
He hung on to my neck...
snuck up to my lips,
breathed into my mouth
and kissed me saying,
"You are mine forever...!"

- *Cassidy Arkin*

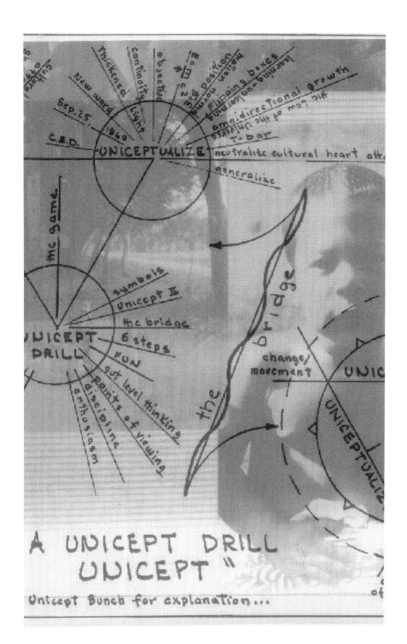

A UNICEPT DRILL
UNICEPT "

Unicept Bunch for explanation...

FROM THE JUNGLE

Dear Cassidy, a foster mother at school told me
she is taking care of a five-year old who has
been through more than anyone can ever tell.
When the child was hungry, her mother would
pour sugar on the floor and make her lick it
up. She didn't know the use of a toilet, just shat
on the floor. The social worker said placing her
in the foster home was like plucking an animal
from the jungle and putting her in civilization.
She didn't know how to talk or use furniture
properly. Yesterday the little girl said to her
foster mother, "Mama, I love you so much!"
The foster mother answered, "I love you too."
Then the five-year-old looked her in the eye
and peed right there on the floor. The wise
foster parent said it was as if she were saying,
*Do you love me? If you do, how much of me will
you love?* While the most passionate love
courses through our veins, we systematically
destroy each other. Heavy. I love you so much,
because with you, being honest and clear-eyed
overcomes all the bullshit.

- *Sandra Rogers-Hare*

FORGOTTEN SEAS

Laughter and forgotten dreams.
Too young to know
and too optimistic to understand
if you throw your hand into the air
your only fight is to keep that solid map
and imagery close to you
as your lines,
Your forgotten seas
And hidden histories are patterned,
centered straight,
bent into your heart…
Your future,
And if you look hard enough
you will see those who went before you,
your bloodlines run fast,
evenly through your flesh.
And here we are reborn,
In my heart.

- *Cassidy Arkin*

FORTUNATE,
I WAS BORN HIGH

Dear Cass,

Harold and I saw "Slam" tonight.
You were right.
It MUST be seen.
I get it.
Fortunate, I was born high,
Living those same vicissitudes.
The experience,
a colloidal obelisk
A disk
Slicing like a boomerang
My life
Sliced
In time,
Forwards behind backwards
This is why,
you must write
This is why as long as you don't express
yourself in writing
You are not living.
Even if your writing is not with a pen or pencil
or computer.
Even if your writing is not with a poem a song
or a film.
Even if your writing is just your young.
Your children,
As mine is.

I love you!

- *Sandra Rogers-Hare*

HUNGRY STARS

We once walked the same path.
You lived one life,
I another.

You lost a soul and died on living.
Soft and hungry are your stars.
Waiting to catch you,
Fly!

- *Cassidy Arkin*

MOM'S UNUSUAL POEM

Geez, get out of that puddle!
You're not strange, but you ARE quintessentially
unusual --
Unusually honest
Unusually brave
Unusually beautiful
Unusually sensitive
Unusually willing to yearn for things everyone
tells you cannot have.

Xoxo,
Mom

RAINBOWS & WINGS

Deep within us—is a connection
to our evolution...
in color.

- *Cassidy Arkin*

ENTHEOS

Dear Cass, just remember, Mother Theresa felt most of her time on this earth that she couldn't connect with entheos, her enthusiasm, her God within. She asked, *God, where are you? Is life worth living?* She ploughed on, doing good work, making others feel better. That is all we know. We are simple creatures finding our way along a dimly lit path in the middle of dark and muddled mountains. We can only see a few steps in front of us and have no idea of the angels and devils flying around us. "Lo, though I walk through the valley of the shadow of death, I shall fear no evil." If you are really in touch with how alone, how solitary each of us is, you have no choice but to continue putting one step in front of the other and rejoicing at anything at all you see that is beautiful...

- Sandra Rogers-Hare

EXIST...

There's going to be a time
when you have no home.
When the sun
leaves for Saturn.
And Dark is a place.
Don't let it deaden you...
Cause is now
Life is now
You're here now
You have life.

- *Cassidy Arkin*

LET THE
FRAGILE
SIDE OF ME
ALWAYS
LIVE IN
STRENGTH

CASSIDY ARKIN

REAL LIFE...

I was living in a
complicatedly structured world,
everything off at an angle and very little
—no options I preferred to take.

I wanted a normal family,
but I realized this crazy world
is the real thing.
It's my life.

- *Sandra Rogers-Hare*

WIDE WORLD

Here ...
where the trees are kings,
and the sea breathes.
The sun walks
And animals dance
the magic of life...
The unfolding story...
The *Wide World*!

- *Cassidy Arkin*

ETERNITY BOUND

"A GUIDE TO SYNANON"

SYNANON || was the first successful drug rehab program for heroin addiction. It was founded by Chuck Dederich, an alcoholic who guided and ran Synanon and its growing population of recovering drug addicts. Its defining innovation was a group interaction called 'The Game," a form of required community therapy.

THE SYNANON GAME || was the engine of Synanon. It was a highly social interaction, an ongoing, engaging practice. The goal was to establish truths that would be upheld and enforced by the entire community through serious examination. It challenged members to examine their behaviors and face the consequences of that behavior in a brutally honest, confrontational way. What was said in the Game was left in the Game.

THE SYNANON PEOPLE || Synanon was first populated by hope-to-die dopefiends, criminals sent by the courts. Then, fashionable characters with various disorders, philanthropists, educators and urban professionals—all contributed something of value to Synanon. In 1968, Synanon began accepting 'Squares,' or non-addicts, if they could pay their way.

THE MOTHER FIGURE OF SYNANON || Betty D was the mother figure of Synanon. Chuck married Betty D in part because she was Black and an ex-addict to demonstrate to the rest of the community that you could marry anybody and make it work. Their marriage transformed Synanon from a bare-bones drug rehab program into a trendy, innovative, inclusive community.

CASSIDY'S PARENTS || Sandy and Ed, both 'Squares,"—nonaddicts, threw themselves wholly into the community. They married, moved into Synanon, brought their piano, lamps, cars and their dog in with them. They helped build the vision of this new community. Unlike the Synanon model for dopefiends, which was to cut off contact with families, friends, and their lives on the outside, Ed and Sandy incorporated Synanon with their outside world.

SYNANON'S EVOLUTION || Synanon differentiated itself from other drug rehab programs when it evolved into a utopian society. The organization grew richer, and more resourceful. Members renovated old factories into posh communal houses and bought huge ranch-lands where they erected whole villages. They purchased fleets of cars, motorcycles, boats and airplanes—all available for any qualified resident's personal use. Synanon had its own schools and stores, its own gyms. They pooled their assets and soon attracted newcomers with considerable capital to buy and develop new Synanon properties, including the Tomales Bay, Ranch, and Walker Creek facilities, in West Marin County to house the expanding Synanon community in a rural setting. They set out to construct a better version of the outside world inside a carefully designed micro-community—a Utopia. They hoped that the world would become one big Synanon family.

The
Miss
19
(The As
Chica

SYNANON JOBS || Synanon expanded its ventures into the business world, starting what became known as ADGAP (Advertising Gifts and Promotions). ADGAP grew into a multi-million-dollar sales force within its first year. Synanon members were quite good at "hustling" even though they were expected to work for free. Soon, Synanon made enough money to support its growing membership in communal-style.

UTOPIA || Many people continued to find deep meaning and a sense of purpose in the Synanon lifestyle, in which every member contributed something of value; it was a social movement. Its members provided each other with laundry services, cafeteria-style dining, and shared housing with doors to personal homes that were always unlocked. The work week was made flexible, and the workday manipulated to fit the needs. Many jobs were shared on innovative schedules, e.g., ten-days-on, ten-days-off. Personal growth was encouraged in off time. Residents could play in the jazz band, paint, sculpt, or study. Meanwhile, the perceived conflict with the outsiders' worldview sharpened most members' sense of dedication to the Synanon community.

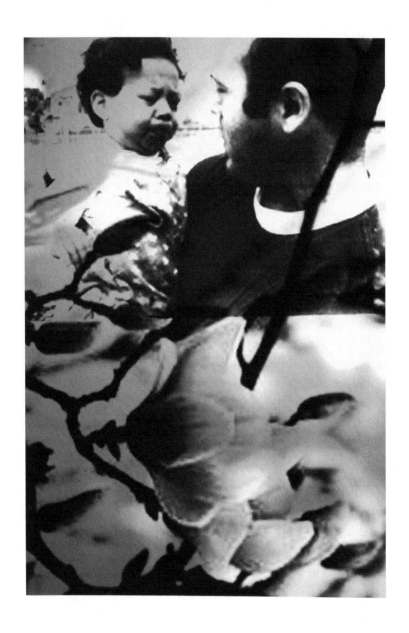

CASSIDY'S BIRTH | | When Cassidy was born, everyone thought she was a clone of her mother. They looked alike, moved alike, and even thought alike. It was as though there was still an invisible umbilical cord that connected them. It was this natural closeness that enforced the group's conviction that Cassidy was indeed a child of Synanon, and she became the focus of commentary and discussion about what born and bred Synanon kids could become. Cassidy was purposely conceived through artificial insemination with the knowledge and cooperation of her entire community, and they referred to her as an original Synanon child.

THE SYNANON SCHOOL | | Cassidy's mother helped design and build the Synanon School. Its purpose was to provide a higher-quality of life and learning than found in the outside world's nuclear family, which had parented the drug addicts, alcoholics, character disorders and squares into Synanon. The Children's Village, was created to separate the children from the dopefiends, who were viewed as an unfavorable influence. As a result, the children were deliberately sequestered in their own community on the 1300-acre, Walker Creek Ranch.

SYNANON PUNK SQUAD | | Troubled kids were sent to Synanon and enrolled in the Punk Squad at the Ranch. This model was used for children of intermediate grades and up. These kids had behavior issues, problems with the law and drug difficulties. They lived together, regulated under a military style to get them in order and in sync with Synanon and the Game. Techniques used on these kids were sometimes brutal. If they disobeyed orders, some were beaten or terrorized and then later Gamed to set an example, a combination of physical, emotional, and mental punishment. When the Punks grew old enough—14 or 15 years old, they joined the Boot Camp.

THE DOWNFALL || started in 1976 and ended in 1988. Chuck, its founder and leader, became more and more unhinged. When the press published exposés some true and some not, Synanon initiated a blizzard of lawsuits, some successful, most frivolous. The press responded almost universally with hard-hitting investigative reporting. Increasingly, opponents turned to criminal courts to prosecute claims against Synanon, who, in turn, filed a lawsuit for $70 million against Time Magazine. Cornered in their own world, members became increasingly uneasy. Synanon reacted at times violently toward those who left and against neighbors. Synanon created its own unit of security guards dressed in black uniforms and carrying semiautomatic weapons. Cassidy and the other children were trained to march military style, and to sit and stand at attention, on command. The resemblance to a military organization was real—Synanon wanted to reflect a military presence. Soon after, the worldwide press described Synanon as a reclusive, militaristic cult. The community had abandoned its founding principles. The arming of the community and the increasing paranoia was the beginning to the end.

THE FINAL DAYS || During the years 1976 to 1991, Synanon became fear motivated—including extreme practices, shaving members' heads, enforced uniforms, changing of partners (mass divorce), violence toward outsiders, gun purchases, the training of a private security guard, naked weigh-ins as part of a fat-a-thon drive, and vasectomies for males over five years' residence. Eventually corporal punishment that had only been used as a last resort for kids who were

79

out of control was applied to the square children as well, actions leading to a growing isolation from the outside world.

LEAVING SYNANON | | By the mid '70's, it had become evident to those on the outside and certain members on the inside, like Cassidy's mother, that Synanon was no longer the idyllic place it was originally conceived to be. As a result, in 1980, Cassidy's mother, Sandy, made the brave and risky choice to leave this once harmonious community and move to Oakland, California with her daughter. Cassidy would soon face a completely new and unfamiliar world. She had spent her formative years in a place modeled after some false, Utopian ideals, but she found America was no Utopia, either.

CONCLUSION | | In the end, the place and the culture in which Cassidy was born became a continual source of controversy. Synanon slowly unwound under financial burdens, along with a slew of legal problems, and was ultimately shut down by the IRS in 1991. Rumored to suffer from bipolar disorder Chuck Dederich fell sick and began drinking again. He moved to a trailer park in Visalia, California with his then wife Ginny where he died in 1997 at the age of 83. Synanon, like so many other societal innovations, was generations ahead of its time, and as with other Utopian dreams before and after, Synanon slowly lost sight of what it initially set out to accomplish and crumbled under its own myth.

A Conversation... *between Cassidy Arkin and Sandra Rogers-Hare about the Synanon experience and why it's important to discover... who you are in the Wide World.*

CASSIDY: *Why is it important to have conversations like this—between mothers and daughters?*

SANDRA: It's important to know who you are. Identity isn't a feeling you get by sitting cross-legged and droning, 'OM'. You have to understand the facts of your existence and where you came from in order to make good choices about where you're going. I need to support you as you step forward, our families need to be strong and centered so that when you move ahead you are not moving alone, you are participating in your own universe knowing what all the parts are and the different players in your life play.

CASSIDY: *When you moved in did it feel like it was a social movement or an actual cult?*

SANDRA: It did not feel like a cult at all. My picture of a cult—and I'm sure that it's just a stereotype that people envision of Synanon—but my view is that in a cult everybody nods and smiles, and they all just kind of march around— it's a little bit one-dimensional. Whereas in Synanon we had free speech and the Game, and we had all different levels of activity. While people like me were working outside Synanon, sales people were putting on business clothes selling advertising specialties all over the country. We had a gasoline station, we had all kinds of things going on, so you felt like you were in a real world, a multi-dimensional real world. It wasn't like going into church and leaving the outside world behind, so from my perspective it really wasn't a cult... it was a movement.

CASSIDY: *So, when you and Dad had me, how was that different from raising a child on the outside?*

SANDRA: Well, first, there was a mythology built around your birth—the Immaculate Conception. People referred to you as the first Synanon child, which wasn't strictly true. Other babies were born in Synanon, but you were a fusion of two people who chose to be in Synanon and you were conceived with the process of what Synanon represented and was about, the Game. That being said—one day shortly after you were born, a very successful ex-dopefiend, he had been in Synanon over five years and was no longer considered a dopefiend came to see us. He was the manager of the Synanon property at Tomales Bay, a young guy. He had a form— he wanted me to sign over to Synanon my rights to you. He didn't know that you shouldn't bring up stressful topics to a hormonal woman, especially one who's lactating. I was adamant, wouldn't do it, and he left. Ed said, "Go ahead and sign it, it's not going to hold up in court." Your father was a realist. I think he moved in with one foot outside of Synanon the entire time, knowing he would return to the outside world. Still, I didn't sign it. What I'm saying is, Chuck talked about how Synanon children belonged to Synanon sort of like the way nuns are married to God in the Catholic church. I didn't buy it. My thinking was, my child is my child and we have elected to be a *part* of Synanon. Synanon doesn't own me or you. But I couldn't afford to have an open, explicit battle about it because I didn't want to be the target of a bunch of negative gaming and I didn't want anybody going after you. So, I think that was sort of the beginning of my insurrection, fighting for my own autonomy, my independence, my own way of doing things and my own daughter.

84

CASSIDY: *Once the downfall started and you were watching your friends, your marriage slip away, suddenly you started to experience the drastic changes in the movement. You were divorced. It came to a point where you decided, this is not good for me or my daughter. What was that moment that changed it all?*

SANDRA: When there are things troubling me— and, all this stuff in Synanon *was* troubling me. From the time you were a couple of weeks old and I was asked to sign you over to Synanon, it was just wordless. I don't handle internal conflicts verbally. I think it's my way of avoiding the enormity of what I am wrestling with. So, I wasn't thinking explicitly about it. There wasn't a specific incident except, as you got close to your sixth birthday, I realized I did not want you going to school in Synanon anymore. It was too insular, too limited. My sense of what it means to be an educator is, you open up the world to kids, you don't close it around them. So, I wanted you in a public school. I wanted you to meet all kinds of people—fat, skinny, tall, purple—all kinds of people. It was sort of like, 'Okay, now we've fooled around enough." You had an excellent infant program, an excellent nursery school, but when it came time to start first grade, I realized I had to take you out. This decision was made knowing that at that point I had no money, no possessions. I had no job, no car. I had no friends in the Bay Area because I had been exclusively involved with Synanon for 15 years. My mother was in Wisconsin. She didn't have the money to relocate me. I was thinking about doing the impossible, but I knew it was time to leave.

CASSIDY: *When we first left Synanon what was that new world like to you, except this time you had me with you?*
SANDRA: At first, it was thrilling. You remember, I was a poor kid raised on the colorless streets of New York City. In California, poverty is more colorful but not really very different. We lived in East Oakland where there was a lot of violence and a lot of rough people. But I felt great. I felt at home, as though I was part of the proletariat again. You went to public school. Everything was wonderful until a couple of months after we left Synanon. Remember, we were living in a terrible, crime-ridden neighborhood. A man in the house directly in front of us shot his wife in the head and killed her. That was too close to home. It was too random, too violent. We managed to get an apartment manager's job in San Leandro, which is a quiet kind of Norman Rockwell-type of town. People grew flowers in their yards, and you walked at the marina, there was blue sky, and everything was nice. But San Leandro was also a racist town. I didn't realize it when we moved in, but realtors red-lined the sale of property so Black people couldn't buy homes there. I also didn't know when I was refused a teaching job by the San Leandro Unified School District that they had never hired a black teacher. I was finally hired by Hayward Unified, which is very diverse. All I knew was that our home had grass and a magnolia tree in the front yard, and people didn't get shot at night. That was enough.

CASSIDY: *What were some of your hopes and fears for me growing up in this New World?*

SANDRA: Well let's not say New World, let's say Wide World. We moved into the Wide World. And at first, I really thought you would be like one of the thousands of kids I had taught, that you would be a normal little kid. You'd get your education and go to college and you'd become a nurse or a teacher or whatever. I didn't realize you were my daughter and you were kind of kinetic, kind of crazy and kind of random and that you were a diverse thinker like me. I didn't realize that. So, thinking that you would just be a normal, predictable kid... I had no fears for you. I thought everything was going to be just peachy. I worked my butt off for our family. I worked two jobs and made sure you went to soccer practice and that my mom sewed you the most beautiful clothes— you were the best-dressed kid in your class— I French-braided your hair. I wasn't afraid for you at all— until later, when you started taking risks, started really living.

FREE

I do feel different... Free.

- Cassidy Arkin

CASSIDY ARKIN || PERSONAL STATEMENT

From the time that I can remember, my dream was to tell my story about being a little brown girl born in a Utopian experiment. As a woman of color, I learned early on there is no entitlement. Nor should there be. I had to seek out those doors of opportunity, and when a door wouldn't open, I'd kick it down. Fortunately, I wear steel-toe heels! I found an outlet and a voice in high school as an on-air television producer when I became involved in a public access television show called, *Cutaway*, a news magazine program for teens that aired in East Bay, California, and was nominated for a California Emmy. That jump-started everything in my dreams. I realized *I can make a difference!* New York City was next. I went East with my dreams and my steel-toe heels. There were many exhausting, lean years pursuing my path, barely making enough money to eat or pay rent. But when you are doing the thing you love, nothing gets in your way or, actually, everything will get in your way, and therein lies the challenge. Being able to tell my story suggests that in the future, things don't have to be the way they've always been. It is a step in a different direction, a step toward women of color like me having multiple opportunities to succeed. I'm here today representing all the little brown girls out there who are pursuing their dreams. My dream is far from realized, but every day I am getting closer.

ABOUT THE AUTHORS

Cassidy Arkin has been working in broadcast television and media as a producer and director for over two decades. From an early age she was a resident of the world where she travelled, studied and worked throughout Europe, primarily in Russia, England, Spain and France. These experiences led her to where she is today. She is a published author and producer for her major project entitled, *Little Brown Girl,* which she co-authored with her mother, Sandra Rogers-Hare. She is an active member of the Producers Guild of America. Independently, she serves as a consultant on behalf of various groups, working to bring media education and design experience to New York City high school students. She admittedly does not lack for perseverance and credits her mother, Sandra Rogers-Hare an educator of over 45 years with instilling in her to keep it true. They have, in many ways, led parallel journeys, separated only by time. But in their separate quests, they have relied on each other to overcome challenges and tell their story. Their work is original and profound and has cross-generational impact.

Sandra Rogers-Hare. After 45 years, Sandra decided to shed the starched underpinnings she had acquired as a teacher and principal and spend the third trimester of her life being an artist. She asserts there is no previous indicator of talent— she just likes the process. She joined a writers' workshop and started writing. Soon, she had enough pieces to create several books, which she mostly gave to members of her family. Sandra loves to travel, take photographs, and read about history. Recently, she has been interested in street murals and the stories they represent. In 2017, she published a memoir on Amazon, *Salmagundi, The Story of a Mixed Race Child in New York and Minnesota.* Her next book, *Synanon, Living in Utopia,* will be published in 2020. Sandra has two children, three stepchildren, five grandchildren and four canine grandchildren. She lives in San Leandro and works diligently as the founder of the Ghenghis Khan Urban Guerrilla Research Society.

Made in the USA
Middletown, DE
25 October 2023

41288359R00053